I0008309

Understanding
Artificial Intelligence
and
Machine Learning

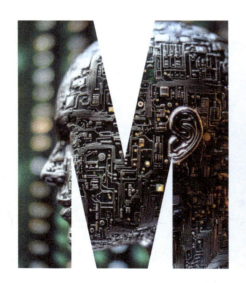

Table of Contents

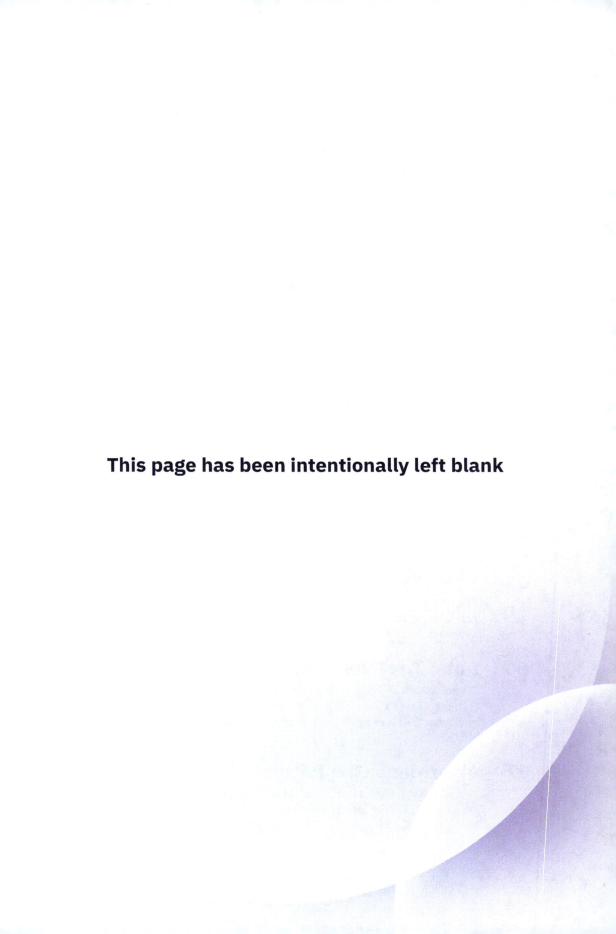

This page has been intentionally left blank

This page has been intentionally left blank

Introduction

Welcome to "Understanding AI and Machine Learning: A Beginner's Guide"

Artificial Intelligence (AI) and Machine Learning (ML) are two of the most exciting and transformative fields in technology today. Whether you've heard about AI from news headlines, movies, or through the buzz in the tech industry, you might be wondering: What exactly is AI? How does Machine Learning work? And what does it all mean for the future?

This book is designed for those who are curious but may feel overwhelmed by the technical jargon often associated with these subjects. You don't need a background in computer science or math to understand the basics of AI and Machine Learning. Here, we will break down complex concepts into simple, digestible explanations, using relatable examples to make the learning process easy and enjoyable.

Author: Jay Julius
Publish date: 11. 09. 2024

This page has been intentionally left blank

What is Artificial Intelligence (AI)?

Artificial Intelligence

Artificial Intelligence (AI) refers to the ability of a machine or computer system to mimic human intelligence processes, such as learning, problem-solving, reasoning, perception, and decision-making. In simple terms, AI is about creating machines that can think, learn, and act intelligently —just like humans do, but often at a much faster pace or in ways that humans can not.

At its core, AI is about teaching computers to do tasks that would normally require human intelligence. These tasks may include things recognizing patterns in data, understanding natural language or text, making decisions based on data, or even performing complex problem-solving.

Key Concepts of AI:

✓ MACHINE LEARNING(ML):

- **Machine Learning** is a subset of AI and refers to the idea that computers can learn from experience (i.e., data) and improve their performance over time, without being explicitly programmed for every scenario. In other words, ML algorithms enable computers to automatically learn from past data to make predictions or decisions in new situations.

✓ DEEP LEARNING:

- A more advanced subset of machine learning, **Deep Learning** uses neural networks (which are inspired by the human brain) to process vast amounts of data and solve more complex problems, such as recognizing images, speech, or even generating text. Deep learning is what powers technologies like voice assistants (like Siri or Alexa), image recognition software, and self-driving cars.

CHAPTER 01

✓ NATURAL LANGUAGE PROCESSING (NLP):

- **NLP** involves teaching machines to understand and interpret human language. This includes everything from speech recognition to sentiment analysis, chatbots, and language translation. It's the technology behind tools like Google Translate or customer service bots.

✓ COMPUTER VISION:

- **Computer Vision** allows machines to "see" and interpret the world through images or video. It's used in facial recognition, autonomous vehicles, and medical imaging.

✓ ROBOTICS:

- AI in **Robotics** combines AI algorithms with physical robots to enable them to perform tasks that require human-like dexterity, decision-making, and sensory perception. Examples include industrial robots, medical surgery assistants, and personal assistants like robotic vacuums.

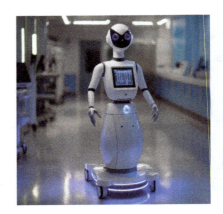

How Does AI Work?

AI systems typically work through a process of training and learning. Here's a simplified breakdown of how this happens:

1 **DATA COLLECTION:**

- AI systems need data to learn. The more data they can process, the better they can "learn." This data might be images, text, sensor readings, or even video footage.

2 **MODEL TRAINING:**

- In machine learning, a model is trained on this data. A model is essentially a mathematical representation of patterns or relationships in the data. The system uses algorithms to identify these patterns and learn from them.

3 **DECISION-MAKING:**

- After training, the AI model can make predictions or decisions based on new, unseen data. For example, a trained AI model for facial recognition can look at a new image and predict whether it contains a specific person.

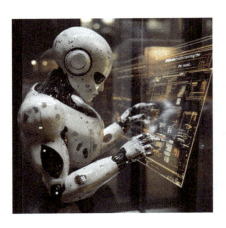

4 **IMPROVEMENT:**

- As the AI system processes more data, it can adjust and improve its model over time. In machine learning, this process is called "training the model," and it helps the system make better and more accurate predictions with each iteration.

Why Does AI Matter?

AI is transforming nearly every industry, making processes more efficient, effective, and scalable. It's being used in areas like:

✓ HEALTHCARE:

- AI helps in diagnosing diseases, analyzing medical images, and personalizing treatment plans.

✓ FINANCE:

- AI algorithms help detect fraudulent transactions, automate trading, and offer personalized financial advice.

✓ ENTERTAINMENT:

- Streaming services like Netflix use AI to recommend shows and movies based on your viewing preferences.

✓ TRANSPORTATION:

- Autonomous vehicles, powered by AI, are making transportation safer and more efficient.

✓ CUSTOMER SERVICE:

- Chatbots and virtual assistants (like Siri and Alexa) use AI to answer questions and solve problems for users.

AI is already deeply integrated into our daily lives, and as technology advances, it will play an increasingly important role in shaping industries, economies, and the way we live.

What is Machine Learning?

Machine Learning

Machine Learning (ML) is a branch of Artificial Intelligence (AI) that focuses on the development of algorithms that allow computers to learn from and make predictions based on data. Unlike traditional programming, where a programmer writes explicit instructions for the computer to follow, in machine learning, the computer learns from data and improves its performance over time without being explicitly programmed for each specific task.

Rather than being programmed with specific instructions for every task, a machine learning model is trained using data, and through this training, it learns how to make predictions or classifications. The more data it processes, the better it gets at making these decisions.

 HOW IT WORKS:

The Learning Process
At its core, machine learning is about recognizing patterns. The process typically involves several steps:

- **Data Collection:** Gathering a large amount of relevant data that the model can learn from. This data can be in various forms, such as numbers, images, or text.

- **Data Preparation:** Cleaning and organizing the data to ensure it is accurate and formatted correctly. This step may involve removing duplicates, handling missing values, and converting data types.

- **Model Selection:** Depending on the problem you're trying to solve (e.g., classification, regression, clustering), you choose an appropriate machine learning model. Models could include decision trees, neural networks, or support vector machines (SVMs).

- **Model Training:** Feeding the prepared data into a machine learning algorithm. The algorithm processes the data and learns to make predictions or decisions based on it.

- **Model Evaluation:** Testing the model with a new set of data (the test set) to see how well it performs. This helps determine if the model can make accurate predictions on data it hasn't seen before.

- **Model Improvement:** Based on the evaluation results, adjustments can be made to the model or the data to enhance its accuracy.

- **Deployment:** Once you're satisfied with the model's performance, it's deployed into production, where it can make real-time predictions or decisions based on new data.

Types of Machine Learning

Types of Machine Learning

Machine Learning (ML) can be categorized into several types based on how the algorithms learn from data. Understanding these types is crucial as they apply to different problems and scenarios. The three primary categories are **supervised learning**, **unsupervised learning**, and **reinforcement learning**.

 SUPERVISED LEARNING:

Supervised learning is the most common type of machine learning. In this approach, the model is trained using labeled data, which means that each training example comes with an output label. The goal is to learn a mapping from inputs to outputs so that when new, unseen data is introduced, the model can accurately predict the label.

 HOW IT WORKS:

 TRAINING PHASE:

- The algorithm learns from the labeled dataset by adjusting its parameters to minimize the difference between its predictions and the actual labels.

 PREDICTION PHASE:

- After training, the model can make predictions on new, unlabeled data based on what it learned.

 EXAMPLE

 EMAIL SPAM DETECTION:

- The model is trained on a dataset of emails labeled as "spam" or "not spam." It learns the characteristics of each category and can then classify new incoming emails.

CHAPTER 03

 IMAGE CLASSIFICATION:

- In this case, a model is trained on labeled images (e.g., pictures of cats and dogs). Once trained, it can classify new images as either a cat or a dog.

→ **KEY ALGORITHMS:**

- ✓ **LINEAR REGRESSION**
- ✓ **LOGISTIC REGRESSION**
- ✓ **DECISION TREES**
- ✓ **SUPPORT VECTOR MACHINES (SVM)**
- ✓ **NEURAL NETWORKS**

You will learn more in details about these algorithms in the later chapters.

CHAPTER 03

 UNSUPERVISED LEARNING

Unsupervised learning deals with unlabeled data. The objective is to identify patterns, groupings, or structures within the data without prior knowledge of what the outputs should be. This type of learning is useful for exploratory data analysis.

 HOW IT WORKS:

- The algorithm examines the data and finds hidden structures or clusters without being given explicit instructions on what to look for.

 EXAMPLE

 CUSTOMER SEGMENTATION:

- Retailers can use unsupervised learning to analyze purchasing behavior and group customers based on similarities. For example, they might find clusters like "bargain hunters" and "loyal customers," helping tailor marketing strategies to each segment.

ANOMALY DETECTION:

- Unsupervised learning can identify unusual data points in a dataset, which is useful in fraud detection. For instance, a bank might use it to flag transactions that deviate significantly from a customer's typical behavior.

CHAPTER 03

KEY ALGORITHMS:

- ✓ K-MEANS CLUSTERING

- ✓ HIERARCHICAL CLUSTERING

- ✓ PRINCIPAL COMPONENT ANALYSIS (PCA)

- ✓ T-DISTRIBUTED STOCHASTIC NEIGHBOR EMBEDDING (T-SNE)

CHAPTER 03

 REINFORCEMENT LEARNING

Reinforcement learning (RL) is inspired by behavioral psychology. In this paradigm, an agent learns to make decisions by interacting with an environment. It receives feedback in the form of rewards or penalties based on its actions, enabling it to learn optimal strategies over time.

 HOW IT WORKS:

 AGENT:

- The learner or decision maker (e.g., a robot or software).

 ENVIRONMENT:

- Everything the agent interacts with.

 ACTIONS:

- Choices made by the agent.

 REWARDS:

- Feedback received from the environment after taking an action, which can be positive or negative.

 EXAMPLE

 GAME PLAYING:

- RL has been famously used to train AI to play games like Chess and Go. The AI learns optimal moves through trial and error, receiving rewards for winning and penalties for losing.

 ROBOTICS:

- In robotics, an agent (robot) learns to navigate an environment (like a maze) by receiving rewards for successfully reaching the end and penalties for hitting obstacles.

CHAPTER 03

KEY ALGORITHMS:

- ✓ Q-LEARNING
- ✓ DEEP Q-NETWORKS (DQN)
- ✓ PROXIMAL POLICY OPTIMIZATION (PPO)
- ✓ ACTOR-CRITIC METHODS

CHAPTER 03

⚛ SUMMARY OF DIFFERENCES

Feature	Supervised Learning	Unsupervised Learning	Reinforcement Learning
Data Type	Labeled data	Unlabeled data	Interaction data
Goal	Predict output based on input	Find patterns and structures	Maximize cumulative rewards
Example	Email classification	Customer segmentation	Game playing
Learning Approach	Direct feedback	No explicit feedback	Trial and error

Understanding the types of machine learning is essential for choosing the right approach to a given problem. Supervised learning is ideal for prediction tasks with labeled data, unsupervised learning is suited for exploratory analysis, and reinforcement learning is effective for decision-making in dynamic environments. By knowing these distinctions, you can better apply machine learning techniques to real-world scenarios.

How Machine Learning Works?

How Machine Learning Works?

Machine learning (ML) is a systematic approach that involves several key steps. Understanding these steps helps demystify how machines learn from data and make predictions or decisions. This chapter outlines the typical workflow in machine learning, breaking it down into five main stages: data collection, data preprocessing, model training, model evaluation, and model improvement.

 DATA COLLECTION

The first step in any machine learning project is gathering relevant data. The quality and quantity of data are critical because they directly impact the model's performance.

 SOURCES OF DATA:

✓ **PUBLIC DATASETS:**

- Many organizations and research institutions provide free datasets for training models (e.g., UCI Machine Learning Repository, Kaggle).

✓ **WEB SCRAPING:**

- Tools can extract data from websites for specific needs.

✓ **API'S:**

- Application Programming Interfaces can be used to fetch data from online services (e.g., Twitter API for tweets).

✓ **SURVEYS AND EXPERIMENTS:**

- Gathering data through user surveys or controlled experiments can provide targeted datasets.

CHAPTER 04

If you want to build a model to predict housing prices, you might collect data from real estate websites, including features like square footage, location, number of bedrooms, and past sale prices.

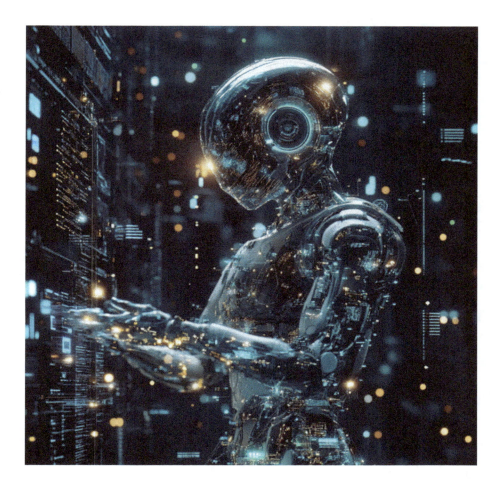

CHAPTER 04

 DATA PREPROCESSING

Once the data is collected, it needs to be cleaned and prepared for analysis. This stage ensures that the data is suitable for training a model.

 KEY STEPS IN DATA PREPROCESSING:

✓ **CLEANING:**

- Removing duplicate entries, correcting errors, and handling missing values (e.g., filling in missing data with averages or medians).

✓ **NORMALIZATION:**

- Scaling numerical values to a standard range (like 0 to 1) to ensure that no single feature dominates the learning process.

✓ **ENCODING CATEGORICAL DATA:**

- Converting categorical variables (like color or type) into numerical format using techniques like one-hot encoding.

✓ **SPLITTING THE DATA:**

- Dividing the dataset into training and testing sets, usually with a ratio of about 80% training and 20% testing. The training set is used to train the model, while the testing set evaluates its performance.

 EXAMPLE

In preparing a dataset of house prices, you might remove entries with missing price information, normalize the square footage, and convert the "location" column into a numerical format.

(3) MODEL TRAINING

This step involves selecting a suitable algorithm and training it on the prepared dataset. The algorithm learns from the data by identifying patterns and relationships.

→ TRAINING PROCESS:

⊘ SELECTING AN ALGORITHM:

- Depending on the problem (regression, classification, etc.), you choose an appropriate algorithm. For example, linear regression for predicting prices or decision trees for classification tasks.

⊘ FITTING THE MODEL:

- The algorithm uses the training data to learn. It adjusts its internal parameters based on the input data to minimize the difference between predicted and actual outputs.

⊘ LEARNING:

- The model finds patterns in the data, which may involve adjusting its weights or structures (in the case of neural networks).

EXAMPLE

Using a linear regression algorithm, the model learns how the features of the houses (like square footage and number of bedrooms) relate to their prices by fitting a line through the data points.

4 **MODEL EVALUATION**

After training, it's crucial to evaluate how well the model performs. This is done using the test dataset that the model has never seen before.

→ **EVALUATION METRICS:**

✓ **ACCURACY:**

- The proportion of correct predictions to the total predictions (used in classification tasks).

✓ **MEAN ABSOLUTE ERROR (MAE):**

- The average of absolute differences between predicted and actual values (common in regression tasks).

✓ **F1 SCORE:**

- A balance between precision and recall, useful for imbalanced datasets.

EXAMPLE

If you're predicting house prices, you might use MAE to measure how far off your predictions were from the actual prices in the test set.

CHAPTER 04

 MODEL IMPROVEMENT

Based on the evaluation results, you may need to refine your model to enhance its performance.

→ **IMPROVEMENT TECHNIQUES:**

✓ **HYPERPARAMETER TUNING:**

- Adjusting the parameters that govern the model's architecture or learning process to improve accuracy.

✓ **FEATURE ENGINEERING:**

- Creating new features from existing data that might help improve model performance (e.g., combining square footage and number of bedrooms into a single feature representing overall livability).

✓ **MODEL SELECTION:**

- Trying different algorithms to see if another one performs better on the same dataset.

If the initial model's accuracy is low, you might try a more complex model, like a decision tree or a random forest, or you might tune the hyperparameters to see if that improves the results.

CHAPTER 04

The **machine learning process** is iterative and requires careful attention to each step. Data collection and preprocessing set the foundation, while training, evaluating, and improving the model are essential for achieving accurate predictions. By understanding how these steps work together, you can better navigate the world of machine learning and apply it to various problems.

Data:
The Fuel of AI

Importance of Data in AI

Data is often referred to as the "fuel" of artificial intelligence (AI) and machine learning (ML) because it powers the algorithms that drive these technologies. Without quality data, AI models cannot learn effectively, make accurate predictions, or provide valuable insights. The saying "garbage in, garbage out" highlights that the quality of data directly affects the outcomes produced by AI systems.

Types of Data

Data comes in various forms, and understanding these types is crucial for effective machine learning.

1 STRUCTURED DATA:

This type of data is highly organized and easily searchable. It is often found in relational databases and spreadsheets.

EXAMPLE

Numerical values (like sales figures), dates, and categorical data (like customer names and addresses).

2 UNSTRUCTURED DATA:

Unstructured data lacks a predefined format, making it more challenging to process and analyze. It accounts for a significant portion of the data generated today.

EXAMPLE

Text documents, images, videos, social media posts, and audio files.

3 **SEMI-STRUCTURED DATA:**

This data type falls between structured and unstructured. While it doesn't have a rigid structure, it includes tags or markers to separate data elements.

JSON and XML files that contain information but are not organized in a traditional database format.

Data Sources

There are numerous sources from which data can be obtained. Some common sources include:

✓ **PUBLIC DATASETS:**

- Many organizations and government entities provide access to large datasets for research and analysis (e.g., Kaggle, UCI Machine Learning Repository).

✓ **WEB SCRAPING:**

- Techniques that extract data from websites, useful for gathering large amounts of information automatically.

✓ **API'S:**

- Application Programming Interfaces allow access to data from various online services. For instance, you can use a Twitter API to collect tweets for sentiment analysis.

✓ SURVEYS AND USER INPUT:

- Data collected through surveys or forms filled out by users can provide insights into preferences and behaviors.

✓ IOT DEVICES:

- Internet of Things devices generate vast amounts of data, such as temperature readings, user interactions, and location data.

Data Quality

The effectiveness of machine learning models heavily depends on the quality of the data used for training. Key aspects of data quality include:

✓ ACCURACY:

- Data should be correct and reliable. Errors in data can lead to incorrect conclusions.

✓ COMPLETENESS:

- A complete dataset contains all the necessary information. Missing values can skew results and hinder the model's ability to learn.

✓ CONSISTENCY:

- Data should be consistent across various sources and formats. Inconsistencies can arise from human error or differing data collection methods.

✓ RELEVANCE:

- The data should be pertinent to the problem being solved. Irrelevant data can add noise and reduce model performance.

Data Preprocessing

Before using data in machine learning models, it often needs to be preprocessed. This step is crucial for ensuring that the data is in a suitable format for analysis.

✓ DATA CLEANING:

- Removing duplicates, correcting errors, and handling missing values. For example, if a dataset has incomplete entries for certain attributes, those rows may need to be filled in or removed.

✓ DATA TRANSFORMATION:

- Changing the format or scale of data. This includes normalization (scaling values to a range) and encoding categorical variables into numerical formats.

✓ FEATURE SELECTION:

- Identifying and selecting the most important features (attributes) for model training. This process can help improve model accuracy and reduce complexity.

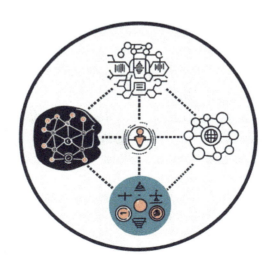

Data Privacy and Ethics

As data plays a crucial role in AI, issues of privacy and ethics have become increasingly important. Collecting and using data responsibly is essential for maintaining trust and compliance with regulations.

⊘ DATA PRIVACY:

- Ensuring that personal information is protected. Regulations like the General Data Protection Regulation (GDPR) in Europe establish strict guidelines on how data should be handled.

⊘ BIAS IN DATA:

- Datasets can reflect societal biases, which may lead to biased AI outcomes. It's essential to ensure that training data is representative and does not perpetuate existing inequalities.

Data is fundamental to the success of AI and machine learning. By understanding the types of data, ensuring its quality, and using it responsibly, organizations can leverage data effectively to build powerful AI systems. The journey from raw data to actionable insights is crucial for unlocking the potential of AI and driving innovation.

Algorithms: The Recipes of Machine Learning

Introduction to Algorithms

In the context of machine learning, algorithms are sets of rules or procedures that guide the learning process. They enable computers to analyze data, identify patterns, and make predictions or decisions. Just as recipes provide instructions for cooking, machine learning algorithms offer structured approaches to solve specific problems.

Categories of Machine Learning Algorithms

Machine learning algorithms can be broadly categorized into three main types based on the learning process and the type of data used: supervised learning, unsupervised learning, and reinforcement learning.

 SUPERVISED LEARNING ALGORITHMS

Supervised learning algorithms are designed to learn from labeled data. Each training example includes an input-output pair, allowing the model to learn the relationship between the two.

Algorithms::
- Linear Regression
- Logistic Regression
- Decision Trees
- Support Vector Machines (SVM)
- Neural Networks

CHAPTER 06

2 UNSUPERVISED LEARNING ALGORITHMS

Unsupervised learning algorithms work with unlabeled data. The goal is to discover hidden patterns or groupings within the data without explicit instructions.

Algorithms::
- K-Means Clustering
- Hierarchical Clustering
- Principal Component Analysis (PCA)
- t-Distributed Stochastic Neighbor Embedding (t-SNE)

3 REINFORCEMENT LEARNING ALGORITHMS

Reinforcement learning algorithms learn through trial and error, interacting with an environment to maximize cumulative rewards. The agent learns to take actions based on the feedback received.

Algorithms::
- Q-Learning
- Deep Q-Networks (DQN)
- Policy Gradients
- Actor-Critic Methods

Choosing the Right Algorithm

The choice of algorithm depends on several factors, including:

✓ **NATURE OF THE PROBLEM:**

- Whether it is a classification, regression, clustering, or reinforcement learning task.

✓ **TYPE OF DATA:**

- Whether the data is labeled or unlabeled, structured or unstructured.

✓ **COMPLEXITY AND INTERPRETABILITY:**

- Simpler algorithms may be preferred for interpretability, while complex algorithms may be required for high accuracy in intricate problems.

Algorithms are at the heart of machine learning, enabling systems to learn from data and make predictions. Understanding the various types of algorithms, their applications, and the contexts in which they thrive is essential for effectively harnessing the power of machine learning. By selecting the right algorithm, practitioners can build robust models that deliver valuable insights and solutions across diverse fields. You will learn about algorithms more in details in the later chapters.

Supervised Learning

Supervised Learning

Supervised learning is one of the most commonly used and foundational techniques in machine learning, enabling algorithms to learn from labeled data in order to predict outcomes for new, unseen data. It is called "supervised" because the learning process is guided by a supervisor—i.e., the model is trained using input data that is paired with known correct outputs (labels). The model learns to map inputs to the correct outputs based on this training data, with the ultimate goal of making accurate predictions.

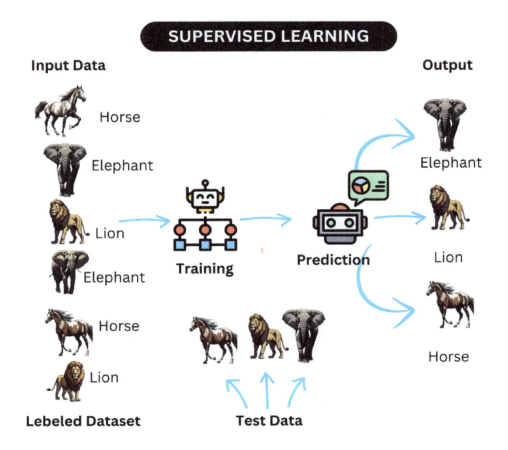

In supervised learning, the training process involves using input-output pairs to guide the algorithm in adjusting its internal parameters (weights or coefficients). After training, the model is expected to generalize well, predicting the correct output for new examples that it hasn't encountered during training.

key components of supervised learning:

1 INPUT (FEATURES)

The input consists of a set of attributes or features that describe each instance. These could be anything from pixel values in an image to measurements of physical quantities in a dataset. The goal of supervised learning is to use these features to predict the output label.

2 OUTPUT (LABELS OR TARGETS)

The output is the value or category that the model is supposed to predict. Depending on the problem, the output could be:
- Discrete values (in classification problems), such as "spam" or "not spam."
- Continuous values (in regression problems), such as predicting house prices or stock prices.

3 TRAINING DATA

Supervised learning requires a labeled dataset for training the model. This dataset includes input-output pairs, where the correct output (label) for each input is provided. The model uses this information to "learn" the relationship between the inputs and the outputs.

4 **TEST DATA**

Once the model is trained, it is tested on a separate set of data, called test data. The test set consists of input-output pairs where the output labels are hidden from the model. This allows us to evaluate how well the model generalizes to new, unseen data.

Process of Supervised Learning

1 **DATA COLLECTION**

The first step in supervised learning is to collect data. This data must contain both input features (independent variables) and corresponding labels (dependent variables or target values). The quality, quantity, and diversity of the data are crucial, as they directly affect the model's performance.

- **Inputs:** These are the features (or attributes) that describe each data point. For example, in a dataset for house price prediction, the features could include the number of rooms, square footage, and neighborhood.

- **Labels:** These are the output values (or target variables) associated with each data point. For instance, in house price prediction, the label would be the price of the house.

EXAMPLE

Suppose you're building a model to predict whether an email is spam. Your dataset would consist of features (e.g., email text, subject, sender) and labels (e.g., "spam" or "not spam").

CHAPTER 07

2 **DATA PREPROCESSING**

Raw data is often noisy and inconsistent, so it must be preprocessed before feeding it into the machine learning model. This step is crucial to ensure that the data is clean, properly formatted, and ready for use.

Common data preprocessing tasks include:

- **Handling Missing Data:** Some data points might have missing values, which could be filled with the mean, median, or mode, or removed if necessary.

- **Normalization/Standardization:** For certain algorithms (e.g., k-NN, SVM), it is important to scale the features so that they have similar ranges, making the learning process more efficient.

- **Encoding Categorical Variables:** If the dataset contains categorical variables (e.g., "red," "blue," "green"), these need to be encoded into numerical values (e.g., one-hot encoding).

- **Splitting the Data:** The dataset is typically divided into two subsets—training data and testing data. A common split is 80/20, where 80% is used for training and 20% for testing. This helps evaluate the model's performance on unseen data.

- **Feature Engineering:** This involves creating new features or transforming existing features to improve model performance. For example, you might combine two features into one or apply a mathematical transformation to a feature.

CHAPTER 07

3　MODEL SELECTION

In this step, you choose an appropriate supervised learning algorithm for the task at hand. The choice of model depends on the type of problem (classification or regression), the size of the dataset, the features available, and the complexity of the problem.

Common models for supervised learning include:

- Linear Regression (for regression problems)
- Logistic Regression (for binary classification problems)
- Decision Trees (for both classification and regression)
- k-Nearest Neighbors (k-NN) (for classification and regression)
- Support Vector Machines (SVM) (for classification)
- Random Forests (ensemble method, for classification and regression)
- Neural Networks (for complex tasks like image recognition, speech recognition)

Each algorithm has its own strengths and weaknesses. For example:

- Decision Trees are easy to interpret but can overfit.
- SVMs are effective for high-dimensional spaces but are computationally expensive.
- Neural Networks can handle large, complex datasets but require substantial computational resources.

CHAPTER 07

4 MODEL TRAINING

Model training is the process where the chosen algorithm learns from the labeled data. During training, the algorithm adjusts its internal parameters to minimize the error in predicting the output based on the input features.

The training process typically involves the following:

- **Feeding Input Data:** The model is presented with input-output pairs (training data) to learn the relationship between inputs and outputs.

- **Loss Function:** The model uses a loss function (or cost function) to evaluate how far off its predictions are from the true labels. For classification, this might be cross-entropy loss, and for regression, it could be mean squared error (MSE).

- **Optimization:** The algorithm uses an optimization technique (like gradient descent) to minimize the loss function. It iterates over the training data, adjusting the parameters (weights) to improve predictions. In neural networks, this might involve backpropagation to adjust the weights in the network.

EXAMPLE

Example: If you're training a decision tree to classify emails as spam or not spam, the model would try to find the best feature splits (e.g., presence of certain words) that minimize classification error.

CHAPTER 07

5 **MODEL EVALUATION**

After training, the model is evaluated on a test dataset that it hasn't seen during training. This step helps assess how well the model generalizes to new, unseen data and gives an indication of its real-world performance.

Evaluation metrics depend on the type of problem:

- **Classification Metrics:**
  - **Accuracy:** The proportion of correct predictions (correct/total predictions).

  - **Precision and Recall:** Precision measures how many of the predicted positives were actually positive, while recall measures how many actual positives were predicted as positive.

  - **F1-Score:** The harmonic mean of precision and recall, useful for imbalanced datasets.

  - **Confusion Matrix:** A table showing true positives, true negatives, false positives, and false negatives.

- **Regression Metrics:**
  - **Mean Absolute Error (MAE):** The average of the absolute differences between predicted and actual values.

  - **Mean Squared Error (MSE):** The average of the squared differences between predicted and actual values.

  - **R-squared:** A measure of how well the model's predictions match the actual values.

The goal is to find a model that performs well on the test set without overfitting to the training data.

6 HYPERPARAMETER TUNING

Once the model is trained and evaluated, the next step is to fine-tune its performance by adjusting the hyperparameters. Hyperparameters are settings that are not learned from the data but are set before training.

These might include:
- Learning rate (for gradient-based optimization)
- Maximum depth of a decision tree
- Number of trees in a random forest
- Number of hidden layers in a neural network
- Regularization parameters (to avoid overfitting)

Techniques for hyperparameter tuning:
- **Grid Search:** Testing a predefined set of hyperparameter values.

- **Random Search:** Randomly selecting hyperparameter values within specified ranges.

- **Bayesian Optimization:** A probabilistic model to optimize hyperparameters efficiently.

7 MODEL VALIDATION

Validation helps ensure that the model has not overfitted to the training data and can generalize well to unseen data. A common technique is cross-validation, where the data is divided into multiple subsets, and the model is trained and evaluated multiple times on different splits to get a more robust estimate of its performance.

K-fold Cross-Validation:
- The data is split into k subsets (or "folds").
- For each fold, the model is trained on the remaining k−1 folds and tested on the current fold.
- The results are averaged to get an overall performance metric.

8 **MODEL DEPLOYMENT**

Once the model has been trained, evaluated, and fine-tuned, it is ready for deployment. The model is then integrated into a real-world application where it can make predictions on new, unseen data.

Steps in deployment:
- **Model Export:** The trained model is exported into a format that can be used for prediction (e.g., .pkl, .h5, or .pb files).

- **Integration:** The model is integrated into the application, such as a web service, mobile app, or software system.

- **Monitoring:** After deployment, the model's performance is monitored to ensure it continues to perform well over time. If the performance drops (e.g., due to changes in the underlying data distribution), the model may need to be retrained.

9 **MODEL MAINTENANCE AND UPDATING**

As new data becomes available, it is important to periodically update the model. This is done to ensure the model adapts to changes in the data (such as concept drift) and maintains its predictive accuracy.

- **Retraining:** Retrain the model with new data periodically or as new patterns emerge.

- **Monitoring:** Continuously monitor the model's performance to identify if it needs updating or improvements.

The process of supervised learning involves several well-defined steps, from collecting and preprocessing data to training, evaluating, and deploying the model. Each step is crucial to ensure that the model performs well on real-world data and can be reliably used for making predictions.

CHAPTER 07

 KEY ALGORITHMS IN SUPERVISED LEARNING:

Supervised learning includes a variety of algorithms, each suited for different types of tasks. Here's a brief overview of some of the most commonly used supervised learning algorithms:

 LINEAR REGRESSION

- **Linear regression** is a statistical method used to model the relationship between a dependent variable (what you want to predict) and one or more independent variables (the features or factors you think might influence the prediction).

How it works:
- It finds the best-fitting straight line (or hyperplane in multiple dimensions) through a set of data points, allowing it to make predictions. The line is determined by minimizing the difference between the predicted and actual values.

Example:
- Predicting house prices based on factors like size, location, and number of rooms. The algorithm tries to find a line that best fits these variables to predict the price.

2 LOGISTIC REGRESSION

- Despite its name, **logistic regression** is used for classification tasks, not regression. It helps predict binary outcomes (two possible categories), such as yes/no or true/false.

How it works:
- Logistic regression uses a function (called the logistic function or sigmoid) to model probabilities. It predicts a value between 0 and 1, which can then be mapped to one of the two categories (for example, 0 could mean "No" and 1 could mean "Yes").

Example:
- Predicting whether an email is spam or not spam, based on features like the sender, subject line, and content.

3 **DECISION TREES:**

- A **decision tree** is a model that makes decisions by splitting data into subsets based on different criteria, much like a flowchart. Each "branch" represents a decision rule, and each "leaf" represents an outcome or prediction.

How it works:
- The tree is built by dividing the data at each step based on a feature that best separates the data, using criteria like "Which feature gives the best split?" (usually based on how well it reduces error or uncertainty).

Example:
- Classifying whether a customer will buy a product or not, based on features like age, income, or browsing history. The decision tree splits the data into smaller groups based on these features until it reaches a prediction.

4 **SUPPORT VECTOR MACHINES (SVM):**

- **Support Vector Machines (SVM)** is a powerful algorithm used for both classification and regression tasks, but it's most commonly used for classification.

How it works:
- SVM works by finding the hyperplane (a line or plane in higher dimensions) that best separates data points into different classes. The algorithm looks for the "maximum margin" between the classes, which means it chooses the hyperplane that maximizes the distance between the closest data points of each class.

Example:
- Classifying emails as spam or not spam. The SVM tries to find a line (or hyperplane) that best separates spam emails from non-spam emails in the feature space.

spam
not spam,

CHAPTER 07

5 NEURAL NETWORKS:

- **Neural networks** are a set of algorithms inspired by the human brain. They are used for both classification and regression tasks and are the foundation for deep learning. Neural networks consist of layers of interconnected "neurons" that process information.

How it works:
- Data is passed through layers of neurons, where each layer performs simple mathematical operations. The final output layer produces a prediction. Neural networks learn by adjusting the weights of connections between neurons, based on the error of their predictions, in a process called **backpropagation.**

Example:
- Recognizing handwritten digits or images (like in image recognition). Neural networks can identify patterns in the data, such as the shape of a digit, and learn to classify it correctly.

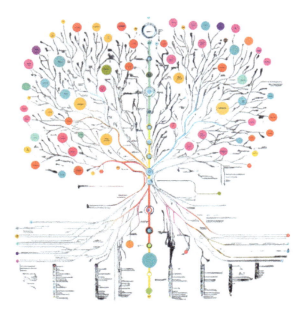

CHAPTER 07

**ADVANTAGES AND DISADVANTAGES OF
SUPERVISED LEARNING**

 ADVANTAGES:

- **Clear Objective:** Supervised learning models have a clear goal — to predict the correct output based on labeled input data.

- **Easy to Evaluate:** Since the output labels are known during training and testing, it's easy to evaluate model performance using standard metrics (e.g., accuracy, error rate).

- **Wide Applicability:** Supervised learning can be applied to a broad range of problems, from classification to regression.

 DISADVANTAGES:

- **Need for Labeled Data:** One of the biggest drawbacks is the need for a large amount of labeled data, which can be time-consuming and costly to obtain.

- **Overfitting Risk:** If the model is too complex, it may overfit to the training data, performing well on the training set but poorly on unseen data.

- **Limited to Historical Data:** Supervised learning models learn from historical data, so they may not adapt well to sudden, unexpected changes in data patterns.

CHAPTER 07

APPLICATIONS OF SUPERVISED LEARNING

Supervised learning is widely used in various fields, including:

- **Finance:** Credit scoring, fraud detection, and algorithmic trading.

- **Healthcare:** Disease diagnosis, medical image classification, and personalized treatment predictions.

- **Retail:** Customer segmentation, recommendation systems, and demand forecasting.

- **Automotive:** Self-driving cars use supervised learning to recognize road signs, pedestrians, and other objects.

- **Natural Language Processing (NLP):** Sentiment analysis, text classification, and machine translation.

Supervised learning is one of the most powerful techniques in machine learning, offering a structured way to train models to make predictions based on labeled data. Its versatility makes it applicable across a wide range of domains, from medical diagnosis to image recognition. By understanding the principles, algorithms, and applications of supervised learning, one can develop efficient and accurate models capable of solving real-world problems.

In the next chapter, we will explore unsupervised learning, where the model learns from data without labels, offering a different approach to machine learning.

Unsupervised Learning

Unsupervised Learning

Unsupervised learning is one of the most important paradigms in machine learning, where the model is trained on data that has no labels. Unlike supervised learning, where the input data comes with corresponding labels (target values), in unsupervised learning, the algorithm works with data that is not labeled, and its goal is to uncover hidden patterns or structures in the data.

In unsupervised learning, the model is tasked with finding the underlying structure or grouping within the input data. This approach is widely used in exploratory data analysis, data mining, and various applications where labeled data is either not available or difficult to obtain.

There are two main categories in unsupervised learning:

- **Clustering:** Grouping similar data points together based on certain features.

- **Association:** Discovering associations or relationships between variables in large datasets.

In unsupervised learning, the model tries to make sense of the data by exploring its structure, such as finding clusters or patterns that were not explicitly labeled.

CHAPTER 08

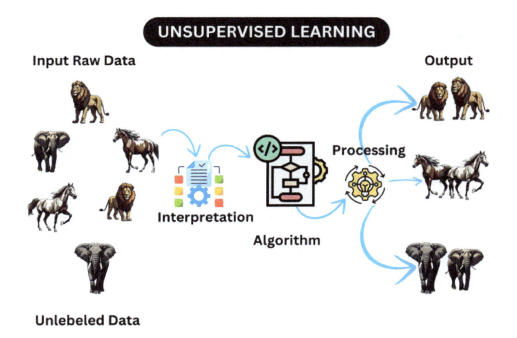

In unsupervised learning, the model tries to make sense of the data by exploring its structure, such as finding clusters or patterns that were not explicitly labeled.

CHAPTER 08

Types of Unsupervised Learning

Unsupervised learning can be broadly categorized into two primary types of tasks:

 CLUSTERING

Clustering is the task of dividing a set of objects into groups (or clusters) based on similarity. The objective is to ensure that objects within a cluster are more similar to each other than to those in other clusters. This is useful when you don't have predefined categories for your data but want to find natural groupings in the data.

Clustering algorithms group similar data points together based on certain features or characteristics. The idea is to find natural groupings within the data, which can be useful in various applications, such as customer segmentation, anomaly detection, or image recognition.

How it works:
- The algorithm identifies similarities between data points.

- It forms clusters where data points within each cluster are more similar to each other than to those in other clusters.

- There are several different clustering methods, such as K-Means, Hierarchical Clustering, and DBSCAN.

Example:
Imagine you have a dataset of customers, including features like age, income, and spending behavior. A clustering algorithm could group these customers into different segments (e.g., high-income spenders, young budget-conscious buyers, etc.) without knowing any labels about the customers beforehand.

CHAPTER 08

✓ APPLICATIONS OF CLUSTERING:

- **Customer Segmentation:** Grouping customers with similar purchasing behavior to personalize marketing efforts.

- **Image Segmentation:** Dividing an image into multiple segments to simplify analysis (e.g., separating foreground from background).

- **Anomaly Detection:** Identifying unusual patterns in data that don't fit the normal structure (e.g., fraud detection).

✓ POPULAR CLUSTERING ALGORITHMS:

1 K-MEANS:

One of the most widely used clustering algorithms. It partitions the data into a predefined number of clusters (k) by minimizing the variance within each cluster.

How it works:
- K-Means is one of the most popular clustering algorithms. It partitions the data into a predefined number of clusters (K). It works by assigning each data point to the nearest cluster centroid and then recalculating the centroid (mean) of each cluster. This process repeats until the centroids stabilize (no more changes).

Key points:
- The algorithm requires the number of clusters (K) to be specified before running.

- K-Means minimizes the sum of squared distances between points and their corresponding centroids.

- Works well when clusters are spherical and roughly of the same size.

CHAPTER 08

2 HIERARCHICAL CLUSTERING:

OBuilds a tree of clusters based on distances between data points, creating a hierarchy of clusters.

How it works:
- Hierarchical clustering builds a tree of clusters (called a dendrogram) by either agglomerating (bottom-up) or dividing (top-down). It starts by treating each data point as its own cluster, then merges the closest clusters iteratively, or starts with all points in one cluster and splits it progressively.

Key points:
- Agglomerative: Start with individual points, merge closest clusters.

- Divisive: Start with all data points in one cluster, recursively split into smaller clusters.

- Does not require the number of clusters to be pre-specified.

- Results in a hierarchical tree structure that can be cut at any level to produce the desired number of clusters.

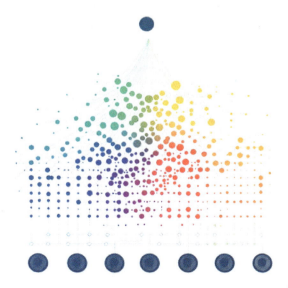

3 **DBSCAN:**

ODBSCAN (Density-Based Spatial Clustering of Applications with Noise) is a density-based algorithm that groups points that are closely packed together and identifies outliers as noise.

How it works:
- DBSCAN clusters data based on density. It defines a cluster as a set of points that are close to each other, with a minimum number of points required in a region for it to be considered a cluster. Points that do not meet this density requirement are labeled as noise.

Key points:
- DBSCAN can find clusters of arbitrary shape, unlike K-Means which works better for spherical clusters.

- It doesn't require the number of clusters to be specified in advance.

- Can handle noise and outliers.

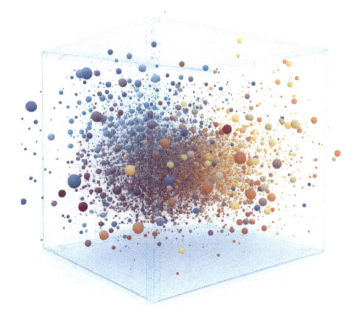

3 GAUSSIAN MIXTURE MODELS (GMM):

A probabilistic model that assumes the data is generated from a mixture of several Gaussian distributions.

How it works:

- GMM is a probabilistic model that assumes the data is generated from a mixture of several Gaussian distributions (normal distributions). It uses the Expectation-Maximization (EM) algorithm to iteratively estimate the parameters of each Gaussian component (mean, variance) and assign probabilities of each data point belonging to each cluster.

Key points:

- Can model clusters with different shapes and sizes (not just spherical).

- Unlike K-Means, GMM assigns probabilities of membership, allowing for soft clustering (a data point can belong to multiple clusters with varying probabilities).

CHAPTER 08

2 **DIMENSIONALITY REDUCTION**

Dimensionality reduction techniques are used to reduce the number of features in a dataset, while preserving the underlying structure or relationships. This is particularly useful when dealing with high-dimensional data (datasets with many features), as it simplifies the model, improves computational efficiency, and reduces overfitting.

Dimensionality reduction techniques aim to reduce the number of features (variables) in the data while retaining as much important information as possible. This is particularly useful when dealing with high-dimensional data (many features), which can be difficult to process and visualize.

How it works:
- The algorithm identifies the most important features (those that explain the most variation in the data).

- It projects the data onto a lower-dimensional space, simplifying it for analysis while preserving key patterns.

- Popular methods include Principal Component Analysis (PCA) and t-Distributed Stochastic Neighbor Embedding (t-SNE).

Example:
In image processing, you might have an image dataset where each image has thousands of pixels as features. Using dimensionality reduction, the model can reduce the number of features (pixels) to a smaller set that still captures the essential characteristics of the images, making it easier to process and analyze.

CHAPTER 08

✓ APPLICATIONS OF DIMENSIONALITY REDUCTION:

- **Data Visualization:** Reducing high-dimensional data to two or three dimensions for visualization in plots.

- **Noise Reduction:** Removing irrelevant or redundant features to improve model accuracy.

- **Preprocessing for other machine learning tasks:** Simplifying data before applying supervised learning models.

✓ POPULAR DIMENSIONALITY REDUCTION ALGORITHMS:

PRINCIPAL COMPONENT ANALYSIS (PCA):

A linear technique that transforms the data into a new coordinate system, where the greatest variances lie along the axes. It is widely used for feature reduction and visualization.

How it works:
- PCA is one of the most widely used dimensionality reduction techniques. It works by identifying the principal components, which are new axes that maximize the variance in the data. These components are linear combinations of the original features. By projecting the data onto the first few principal components, we can reduce the dimensionality while retaining most of the variance in the data.

Key points:
- PCA finds the directions of maximum variance in the data.

- The new components are orthogonal (uncorrelated) to each other.

- It is often used for feature extraction, compression, and noise reduction.

2 T-SNE:

t-Distributed Stochastic Neighbor Embedding (t-SNE) is a non-linear technique that is particularly effective for visualizing high-dimensional data in two or three dimensions.

How it works:

- t-SNE is a nonlinear dimensionality reduction technique that is particularly effective for visualizing high-dimensional data in 2D or 3D. It minimizes the divergence between probability distributions in high-dimensional and low-dimensional spaces, preserving the local structure of the data (i.e., similar points stay close to each other).

Key points:

- t-SNE works well for visualizing clusters and relationships in complex datasets.

- It's often used for visualization of data like images, text, or gene expression.

- t-SNE is computationally expensive and not suited for large-scale datasets.

CHAPTER 08

3 AUTOENCODERS:

A type of neural network used for unsupervised learning to reduce dimensionality by learning a compressed representation of the input data.

How it works:
- Autoencoders are neural networks used for unsupervised learning of efficient representations of data. An autoencoder consists of two parts: an encoder that reduces the dimensionality of the data, and a decoder that reconstructs the original data. The network is trained to minimize the difference between the input and the reconstructed output.

Key points:
- The encoder learns a compressed representation of the input data in a lower-dimensional space.

- Autoencoders can learn both linear and nonlinear transformations.

- Used in conjunction with neural networks for tasks like denoising, compression, and feature extraction.

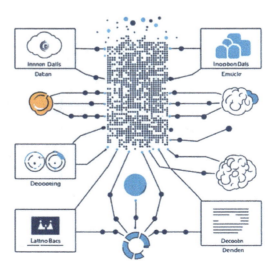

4 INDEPENDENT COMPONENT ANALYSIS (ICA):

Independent Component Analysis (ICA) is a computational technique used in statistics and signal processing to separate a multivariate signal into additive, statistically independent components. ICA is particularly useful for problems where you have mixed signals and you want to recover the original sources (independent components) that contributed to the observed mixture. The key feature of ICA is that it assumes the sources are statistically independent, unlike traditional Principal Component Analysis (PCA), which only focuses on maximizing variance.

ICA is often used in scenarios like blind source separation, where the task is to extract original sources from mixed signals when you don't have access to the sources themselves.

How it works:
- ICA is a technique for separating a multivariate signal into additive, independent components. It's similar to PCA but focuses on statistical independence rather than variance. ICA is particularly useful when dealing with signals or data where components are mixed together, like in blind source separation (e.g., separating audio sources in a recording).

Key points:
- ICA works best when the data contains independent sources mixed together.

- Unlike PCA, which focuses on variance, ICA seeks to make the components as independent as possible.

3 ASSOCIATION RULE LEARNING

Association rule learning is a method used to discover interesting relationships between variables in large datasets. The goal is to find rules that describe how frequently certain events or patterns occur together.

Dimensionality reduction techniques aim to reduce the number of features (variables) in the data while retaining as much important information as possible. This is particularly useful when dealing with high-dimensional data (many features), which can be difficult to process and visualize.

How it works:
- The algorithm identifies the most important features (those that explain the most variation in the data).

- It projects the data onto a lower-dimensional space, simplifying it for analysis while preserving key patterns.

- Popular methods include Principal Component Analysis (PCA) and t-Distributed Stochastic Neighbor Embedding (t-SNE).

Example:
In image processing, you might have an image dataset where each image has thousands of pixels as features. Using dimensionality reduction, the model can reduce the number of features (pixels) to a smaller set that still captures the essential characteristics of the images, making it easier to process and analyze.

CHAPTER 08

✓ APPLICATIONS OF ASSOCIATION RULE LEARNING:

- **Market Basket Analysis:** Discovering items that are often purchased together (e.g., "if a customer buys bread, they are likely to buy butter").

- **Web Page Recommendation:** Recommending pages that are often visited together based on user behavior

✓ POPULAR ASSOCIATION RULE LEARNING ALGORITHMS:

① APRIORI ALGORITHM:

An algorithm used to find association rules by iteratively finding frequent itemsets in the dataset.

How it works:
- The Apriori algorithm finds frequent itemsets in transactional data and generates association rules based on these itemsets. It uses a "bottom-up" approach, starting with individual items and iteratively combining them to form larger itemsets, checking the frequency of their occurrence.

Key points:
- Market basket analysis (e.g., items frequently purchased together)

- Used in recommendation systems and fraud detection.

CHAPTER 08

2 **ECLAT ALGORITHM:**

Another algorithm for frequent itemset mining, using a depth-first search approach.

The **Eclat** (Equivalence Class Transformation) algorithm is a popular algorithm used in association rule mining to find frequent itemsets in a dataset. It is an alternative to the Apriori algorithm and is designed to be more efficient, especially for dense datasets.

How it works:
- The Eclat algorithm is an improvement over the Apriori algorithm for frequent itemset mining. It uses a depth-first search approach and a vertical data format, which can be more efficient for large datasets.

Key points:
- Suitable for finding patterns in transactional data.

- Used in Market basket analysis.

Unsupervised learning offers powerful tools for discovering hidden patterns and structures within unlabeled data. By leveraging various algorithms, practitioners can gain valuable insights across diverse fields, from marketing to healthcare. Understanding the processes, techniques, and challenges associated with unsupervised learning is essential for effectively harnessing its potential.

CHAPTER 08

ADVANTAGES AND DISADVANTAGES OF UNSUPERVISED LEARNING

 ADVANTAGES:

- **No Labeled Data Required:** Unsupervised learning doesn't require labeled data, which reduces the cost and effort of manually annotating datasets.

- **Data Exploration:** Ideal for exploratory data analysis, helping to understand the data distribution and identify features for further supervised learning tasks.

- **Adaptability:** Can handle large amounts of unstructured or unlabeled data, making it suitable for modern, real-world datasets like images, videos, and text.

- **Discover Hidden Patterns::** It can uncover hidden patterns, structures, or relationships within the data that may not be apparent otherwise.

 DISADVANTAGES:

- **Complexity:** Often more challenging to implement and interpret compared to supervised learning, as there is no clear "correct" output to evaluate.

- **Uncertainty in Results:** Outcomes can be ambiguous or inconsistent due to the lack of labeled data for validation and evaluation.

- **Overfitting Risk::** Algorithms may find patterns in noise or irrelevant features, leading to overfitting without proper preprocessing.

- **Scaling Challenges::** Some unsupervised algorithms (e.g., K-means) may struggle with high-dimensional data, requiring techniques like PCA for dimensionality reduction.

Reinforcement Learning

Reinforcement Learning

Reinforcement Learning (RL) is a branch of machine learning where an agent learns how to make decisions by performing actions in an environment to maximize some notion of cumulative reward. Unlike supervised learning, where the model learns from a labeled dataset, RL relies on feedback from the environment in the form of rewards or penalties. This chapter explores the concepts, key components, algorithms, and applications of reinforcement learning.

This type of learning is based on the concept of agents that take actions in an environment to maximize a reward. The agent learns from the consequences of its actions rather than from labeled examples.

The ultimate goal of reinforcement learning is to find the optimal policy, which maximizes the cumulative reward over time.

EXAMPLE

A self-driving car learns to navigate by receiving positive feedback (a reward) for making safe driving decisions and negative feedback (a penalty) for unsafe actions.

Reinforcement Learning can be classified into three types:

- **Policy-based:** This method focuses on finding the best strategy or plan to maximize rewards. It uses clear rules or policies to decide what actions to take.

- **Value-based:** This approach aims to improve how the system evaluates actions by optimizing a value function, which helps predict the best action to take in a given situation.

- **Model-based:** In this method, a virtual version of the environment is created. The agent learns by practicing and testing its actions in this simulated environment before applying them in the real world.

Key Concepts of Reinforcement Learning

- **Agent:** The learner or decision-maker.

- **Environment:** Everything the agent interacts with. It provides feedback based on the agent's actions.

- **State (S):** A representation of the current situation in the environment.

- **Action (A):** Choices available to the agent.

- **Reward (R):** Feedback received after performing an action. It can be positive (reward) or negative (penalty).

- **Policy (π):** The strategy the agent follows to decide the next action based on the current state.

- **Value Function (V):** Measures how good a state is in terms of expected future rewards.

- **Q-Function (Q):** Measures how good a state-action pair is in terms of expected future rewards.

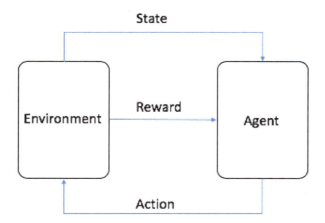

How it works

Reinforcement Learning (RL) operates through a feedback loop where an agent interacts with an environment, observes the results of its actions, and learns over time to make better decisions. Below is a detailed breakdown of the process:

Process of Reinforcement Learning

1 NITIALIZE THE ENVIRONMENT AND AGENT

- The environment represents the problem the agent must solve. It includes the state space (all possible situations) and actions the agent can take.

- The agent starts with little or no prior knowledge about the environment.

2 OBSERVE THE CURRENT STATE (S)

- The environment provides the agent with its current state, which represents the situation the agent is in.

- Example: In a chess game, the state could represent the positions of all the pieces on the board.

3 CHOOSE AN ACTION (A)

- The agent selects an action based on a policy (π), which is a strategy that maps states to actions.

- Initially, the agent explores randomly because it has no knowledge of the environment (exploration).

- Over time, the agent balances between:
  - Exploration: Trying new actions to gather more information.

  - Exploitation: Choosing actions known to yield high rewards based on past experience.

4 PERFORM THE ACTION IN THE ENVIRONMENT

- The chosen action is executed, and the environment changes in response to the action.

- Example: In a self-driving car, turning left or accelerating changes the car's position.

5 RECEIVE A REWARD (R)

- The agent receives a reward, which is a numerical signal indicating the quality of the action.

- The agent's goal is to maximize the cumulative reward over time..

- Rewards can be:
  - **Immediate:** Given right after the action (e.g., winning a point in a game).

  - **Delayed:** Occurring after a sequence of actions (e.g., winning the game after several moves).

6 OBSERVE THE NEW STATE (S')

- After taking the action, the agent transitions to a new state, which reflects the updated situation of the environment.

7 UPDATE THE POLICY OR Q-VALUE

- The agent updates its policy or value function using the new information from the environment:

  - Policy (π): Directly improves the decision-making strategy.

  - Value Function: Estimates the total reward the agent can expect from a state or action.

- If using Q-Learning (a common algorithm):

$$Q(S, A) \leftarrow Q(S, A) + \alpha \left[R + \gamma \max_{A'} Q(S', A') - Q(S, A) \right]$$

Where:
- α: Learning rate.
- γ: Discount factor (how much future rewards matter compared to immediate rewards).
- Q(S,A): Value of taking action A in state S.

8 REPEAT THE PROCESS

- Steps 2–7 are repeated until the agent learns an optimal policy to maximize cumulative rewards.

- The agent continually improves by trying different actions and learning from their outcomes.

CHAPTER 09

Training a Robot to Walk:

- **State:** The robot's current posture, position, or speed.

- **Action:** Adjusting the angle of joints or speed of motors.

- **Reward:** Positive reward for moving closer to the goal or staying balanced; negative reward for falling.

- **Process:**
  - Initially, the robot stumbles and falls as it tries random actions (exploration).
  - Over time, it learns which movements lead to walking successfully (exploitation).

✓ APPLICATIONS OF REINFORCEMENT LEARNING:

- **Robotics:** Training robots to perform tasks such as grasping objects, navigating environments, and interacting with humans. RL enables robots to learn through real-world experiences.

- **Game Playing:** Developing AI agents that can play video games or board games, often achieving superhuman performance. Examples include AlphaGo, which defeated human champions in the game of Go.

- **Autonomous Vehicles:** Enabling self-driving cars to learn safe driving strategies by interacting with their environment, including other vehicles and pedestrians.

- **Finance:** Optimizing trading strategies by allowing agents to learn from market conditions and historical data, adapting to changing environments.

- **Healthcare:** Personalizing treatment plans by training models to optimize patient outcomes based on individual responses to treatments.

CHAPTER 09

✓ POPULAR REINFORCEMENT LEARNING ALGORITHMS:

1 Q-LEARNING

- **Type:** Value-Based, Model-Free.

- **Key Idea:** Learn the Q-value (quality) for each state-action pair without requiring a model of the environment.

How it Works:
- The agent updates its Q-values using the Bellman Equation:

$$Q(s,a) \leftarrow Q(s,a) + \alpha \left[r + \gamma \max_{a'} Q(s',a') - Q(s,a) \right]$$

  - α: Learning rate.
  - γ: Discount factor (how much future rewards are valued).
  - r: Immediate reward.
  - s′: Next state.

- The agent iteratively improves its Q-table until convergence.

Example:
- **Scenario:** A robot navigating a grid to reach a goal while avoiding obstacles.

- **Process:**
  a. Start with a Q-table initialized to 0.
  b. The robot explores the grid (e.g., using ε-greedy policy).
  c. Updates Q-values based on the rewards received for each state-action pair.

2 DEEP Q-NETWORKS (DQN)

- **Type:** Value-Based, Model-Free.

- **Key Idea:** Combines Q-learning with deep neural networks to handle large state spaces.

How it Works:
- Instead of a Q-table, a neural network approximates the Q-function.

- Two networks are used:
    1. Q-Network: Estimates Q(s,a)Q(s, a)Q(s,a).
    2. Target Network: Provides stable targets for training.

- **Update rule:**

$$\text{Loss} = \left(r + \gamma \max_{a'} Q_{\text{target}}(s', a') - Q(s, a)\right)^2$$

- The network is trained to minimize this loss.

Example:
- **Scenario:** Playing Atari games.

- **Process:**
    1. The input to the neural network is the game screen (state).
    2. The network outputs Q-values for all possible actions.
    3. The agent selects actions using ε-greedy exploration.

CHAPTER 09

3 **POLICY GRADIENT METHODS**

- **Type:** Policy-Based, Model-Free.

- **Key Idea:** Directly optimize the policy without learning value functions.

How it Works:
- The policy π(a   s;θ) (a probability distribution over actions given states) is parameterized by θ.

- The agent improves the policy by maximizing the expected reward:

$$J(\theta) = \mathbb{E}_{\pi}\big[R\big]$$

- Uses gradient ascent on J(θ):

$$\theta \leftarrow \theta + \alpha \nabla_{\theta} J(\theta)$$

- **Algorithms:** REINFORCE, Actor-Critic methods.

Example:
- **Scenario:** Teaching a robot to balance a pole.
- **Process:**
  1. Start with a random policy.
  2. Perform actions and observe rewards.
  3. Gradually adjust the policy parameters to maximize rewards.

4 ACTOR-CRITIC METHODS

- **Type:** Policy-Based with Value-Based component.

- **Key Idea:** Combines the advantages of value and policy methods.

How it Works:
- Two models are used:
  1. Actor: Learns the policy $\pi(a \mid s;\theta)$.
  2. Critic: Estimates the value function $V(s;w)$.

- The critic helps reduce variance in policy updates by providing feedback.

Example:
- **Scenario:** Continuous control tasks like robot locomotion.

- **Process:**
  1. Actor determines actions.
  2. Critic evaluates those actions and updates the policy.

5 ALPHAGO AND MONTE CARLO TREE SEARCH (MCTS)

- **Type:** Model-Based with Policy and Value learning.

- **Key Idea:** Combines RL with search algorithms to play games like Go.

How it Works:
- Uses MCTS to explore possible future game states.

- Trains a neural network to predict value (win probability) and policy (action probabilities).

Example:
- Scenario: AlphaGo's victory against human Go champions.

- Combines self-play, MCTS, and RL to master complex games.

6   SARSA (STATE-ACTION-REWARD-STATE-ACTION)

- **Type:** Value-Based, Model-Free, On-Policy.

- **Key Idea:** Similar to Q-learning but updates Q-values based on the action actually taken in the next state.

How it Works:
- **Update rule:**

$$Q(s,a) \leftarrow Q(s,a) + \alpha \big[r + \gamma Q(s',a') - Q(s,a) \big]$$

- Uses the action a′ actually chosen in s′, not the one with the highest Q-value.

Example:
- **Scenario:** Same grid navigation as Q-Learning.

- **Difference:** Updates depend on the agent's specific policy, leading to safer exploration in environments with risks.

7   PROXIMAL POLICY OPTIMIZATION (PPO)

- **Type:** Policy-Based.

- **Key Idea:** Optimizes the policy using a clipped surrogate objective to maintain stability.

How it Works:
- Balances exploration and exploitation by constraining policy updates:

$$L^{\mathrm{CLIP}}(\theta) = \mathbb{E}\big[\min(r(\theta)\hat{A}, \mathrm{clip}(r(\theta), 1 - \epsilon, 1 + \epsilon)\hat{A}) \big]$$

- $r(\theta)$: Probability ratio of new to old policy.
- $\hat{A}$: Advantage estimate.

Example:
- **Scenario:** Training an AI agent for complex 3D games.

- **Benefit:** Stable learning with high sample efficiency.

COMPARISON OF ALGORITHMS

Algorithm	Type	Strengths	Weaknesses
Q-Learning	Value-Based	Simple, effective in discrete environments	Struggles with large state spaces
SARSA	Value-Based	Safer exploration	Converges slower than Q-Learning
DQN	Value-Based	Handles large state spaces	Requires significant computational power
Policy Gradient	Policy-Based	Effective for continuous action spaces	High variance in updates
Actor-Critic	Hybrid	Combines value and policy learning	Complex to implement
PPO	Policy-Based	Stable and efficient learning	Requires tuning

Reinforcement learning represents a powerful framework for teaching agents to make decisions through interaction with their environments. By learning from feedback, RL has wide-ranging applications across industries, from robotics to finance. Understanding the key concepts, algorithms, and challenges associated with reinforcement learning is essential for harnessing its potential and developing intelligent systems that can adapt and learn in dynamic settings.

CHAPTER 09

ADVANTAGES AND DISADVANTAGES OF REINFORCEMENT LEARNING

ADVANTAGES:

- **Dynamic Adaptation:** Can adapt to changes in the environment.

- **No Supervised Data Required:** Learns from feedback rather than labeled data

- **Versatility:** Applicable in a wide range of fields, from robotics to natural language processing.

DISADVANTAGES:

- **Data Efficiency:** Reinforcement Learning often requires a large number of interactions to learn effectively.

- **Complexity:** Designing the reward signal and handling large action/state spaces can be difficult.

- **Instability:** Learning can be unstable, especially in environments with delayed rewards or sparse feedback.

Real-World Applications of AI

CHAPTER 10

AI Applications

Artificial Intelligence (AI) has evolved from theoretical concepts to practical tools that are transforming industries and enhancing everyday life. By leveraging machine learning, natural language processing, computer vision, and other AI technologies, businesses are optimizing processes, improving customer experiences, and driving innovation. This chapter explores several key applications of AI in various domains.

Artificial Intelligence (AI) has a wide range of real-world applications across various industries. Here are some key applications explained in detail, with examples:

 HEALTHCARE

AI is transforming healthcare by improving diagnostics, treatment plans, and patient care.

Examples:
- **Medical Imaging and Diagnosis:** AI tools like IBM Watson and Google's DeepMind analyze medical images such as X-rays, MRIs, and CT scans to detect diseases like cancer, fractures, or abnormalities with high accuracy.

- **Personalized Medicine:** AI helps tailor treatments based on a patient's genetic makeup and medical history. For instance, Tempus uses AI to design customized cancer therapies.

- **Virtual Health Assistants:** Chatbots like Ada or Babylon Health provide health advice, answer medical questions, and assist with scheduling appointments.

CHAPTER 10

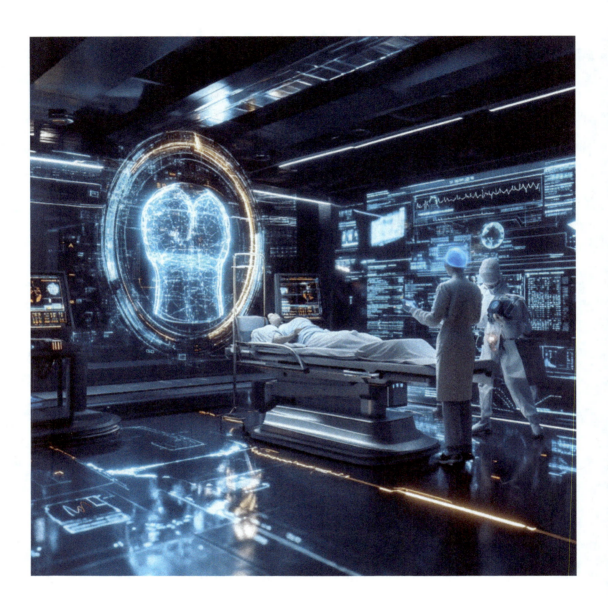

AI is revolutionizing healthcare by improving diagnostics, personalizing treatment plans, and streamlining administrative processes.

CHAPTER 10

2 **FINANCE**

AI is widely used for fraud detection, risk management, and financial advisory services.

Examples:
- **Fraud Detection:** Credit card companies like Visa and MasterCard use AI algorithms to identify suspicious transactions in real-time.

- **Algorithmic Trading:** AI-powered systems analyze market data and execute trades faster and more accurately than humans.

- **Personal Finance Management:** Apps like Mint and Cleo use AI to track spending patterns and offer budget recommendations.

CHAPTER 10

③ RETAIL AND E-COMMERCE

AI enhances customer experiences and streamlines operations in retail.

Examples:

- **Product Recommendations:** Platforms like Amazon and Netflix use AI to recommend products or shows based on user behavior and preferences.

- **Chatbots for Customer Support:** AI-powered chatbots such as Drift or Zendesk provide instant responses to customer queries, improving satisfaction.

- **Inventory Management:** Retailers use AI to predict demand and manage stock efficiently. For instance, Walmart uses AI for supply chain optimization.

CHAPTER 10

 TRANSPORTATION AND LOGISTICS

AI improves safety, efficiency, and reliability in transportation systems.

Examples:
- **Autonomous Vehicles:** Companies like Tesla, Waymo, and Uber use AI to develop self-driving cars that navigate roads and make decisions without human input.

- **Route Optimization:** AI systems like Waze and Google Maps analyze traffic patterns to suggest the fastest routes.

- **Predictive Maintenance:** AI helps airlines and shipping companies predict when vehicles or machinery need repairs, reducing downtime.

 EDUCATION

AI is reshaping how students learn and teachers educate.

Examples:
- **Personalized Learning:** Platforms like Khan Academy and Duolingo use AI to adapt content to the learner's pace and style.

- **Grading Automation:** AI tools like Gradescope assist teachers by automating the grading of exams and assignments.

- **Virtual Tutors:** AI-powered virtual tutors provide additional learning support to students outside classrooms.

CHAPTER 10

6 MANUFACTURING

AI is revolutionizing production processes by enhancing precision and efficiency.

Examples:
- **Predictive Maintenance:** AI systems monitor machinery to predict failures before they occur, saving costs.

- **Quality Control:** AI-powered visual inspection tools identify defects in products during production.

- **Robotics:** Robots equipped with AI are used in assembly lines, such as in car manufacturing by companies like BMW and Toyota.

CHAPTER 10

7 **ENTERTAINMENT**

AI is reshaping the entertainment industry by creating immersive and personalized experiences.

Examples:
- **Content Creation:** AI tools like RunwayML generate music, artwork, or videos. For example, AI is used to create realistic deepfake videos or movie special effects.

- **Game Development:** AI enhances video game realism by creating intelligent non-player characters (NPCs) and dynamic scenarios.

- **Streaming Services:** Platforms like Spotify and YouTube use AI to recommend content based on user preferences.

8 **AGRICULTURE**

AI helps optimize crop production, monitor livestock, and improve resource efficiency.

Examples:
- **Crop Monitoring:** AI-powered drones and sensors monitor crop health and detect diseases.

- **Precision Farming:** AI tools like Blue River Technology use computer vision to identify weeds and apply pesticides selectively.

- **Weather Prediction:** AI predicts weather conditions, helping farmers plan planting and harvesting.

9 **ENERGY**

AI helps in energy conservation, management, and renewable energy optimization.

Examples:
- **Smart Grids:** AI manages electricity distribution efficiently, reducing power outages.

- **Energy Forecasting:** Companies like GE use AI to predict energy demand and optimize power generation.

- **Renewable Energy Management:** AI optimizes solar panel performance and wind turbine efficiency.

CHAPTER 10

10 **SECURITY AND SURVEILLANCE**

AI enhances public safety and security through intelligent monitoring systems.

Examples:
- **Facial Recognition:** AI-based systems like Clearview AI identify individuals for security purposes.

- **Behavior Analysis:** AI monitors video footage to detect unusual activities and alert authorities.

- **Cybersecurity:** AI tools like Darktrace identify and prevent potential cyberattacks.

11 **ENVIRONMENT AND SUSTAINABILITY**

AI contributes to environmental conservation and sustainable practices.

Examples:
- **Wildlife Conservation:** AI analyzes camera trap images to track animal populations and detect poaching.

- **Climate Modeling:** AI predicts climate changes and their impact on ecosystems.

- **Waste Management:** AI-powered robots sort recyclables from waste streams, improving recycling rates.

CHAPTER 10

12 **REAL ESTATE**

AI contributes to environmental conservation and sustainable practices.

Examples:
- **Wildlife Conservation:** AI analyzes camera trap images to track animal populations and detect poaching.

- **Climate Modeling:** AI predicts climate changes and their impact on ecosystems.

- **Waste Management:** AI-powered robots sort recyclables from waste streams, improving recycling rates.

CHAPTER 10

AI's real-world applications span a wide range of industries, enhancing efficiency, improving customer experiences, and driving innovation. As AI technology continues to advance, its impact will likely expand further, offering new solutions to complex challenges. Understanding these applications helps us appreciate the transformative power of AI and its potential to shape the future.

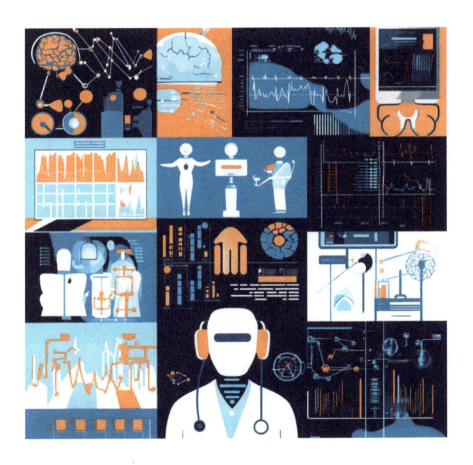

Challenges and Limitations of AI

CHAPTER 11

AI Challenges

While artificial intelligence holds immense potential for transforming industries and improving lives, it also faces several significant challenges and limitations. These issues range from technical hurdles to ethical considerations, impacting the effectiveness and acceptance of AI solutions. This chapter explores some of the key challenges in the field of AI.

 DATA QUALITY AND AVAILABILITY

AI systems rely heavily on data for training and validation. The quality, quantity, and representativeness of this data are crucial for successful AI applications.

Data Quality:
- Inaccurate, biased, or incomplete data can lead to poor model performance and misleading outcomes. Ensuring data quality is essential to building reliable AI systems.

Data Availability:
- Some applications may suffer from a lack of available data, particularly in specialized fields like healthcare or rare events. Limited data can hinder the training of effective models.

Data Privacy:
- Collecting and using personal data raises significant privacy concerns. Organizations must navigate regulations (like GDPR) while ensuring user consent and data protection.

CHAPTER 11

2 **ALGORITHMIC BIAS**

AI systems can inadvertently perpetuate or even amplify existing biases present in the training data. This can lead to unfair outcomes and discrimination.

Sources of Bias:
- Bias can stem from various sources, including unrepresentative training datasets, human biases in labeling, and biased algorithms.

Consequences:

- Biased AI systems can result in unfair treatment in areas such as hiring, lending, law enforcement, and healthcare, leading to societal implications and loss of trust in AI technologies.

3 **INTERPRETABILITY AND TRANSPARENCY**

Many AI models, especially complex ones like deep neural networks, operate as "black boxes," making it challenging to understand their decision-making processes.

Lack of Interpretability:
- Stakeholders may find it difficult to trust AI systems if they cannot understand how decisions are made. This is particularly critical in high-stakes scenarios such as healthcare or criminal justice.

Need for Transparency:
- Increasing demand for explainable AI has led to research into methods that enhance model interpretability, but achieving transparency without sacrificing performance remains a challenge.

CHAPTER 11

 SECURITY AND ROBUSTNESS

AI systems can be vulnerable to various security threats that could undermine their reliability and safety.

Adversarial Attacks:
- Malicious actors can exploit weaknesses in AI models by creating inputs specifically designed to deceive the model (e.g., slightly altered images that mislead image recognition systems).

Data Poisoning:
- Attackers can manipulate the training data, introducing biases or vulnerabilities that compromise the integrity of the model.

Dependence on Infrastructure:
- AI systems often require significant computational resources and stable infrastructure, making them susceptible to disruptions.

Explanation:
AI systems can be vulnerable to hacking, data breaches, and adversarial attacks, posing significant risks to sensitive information and operations.

Example:
In autonomous vehicles, adversarial attacks like tricking a system into misreading stop signs could lead to accidents.

CHAPTER 11

5 ETHICAL AND LEGAL CONSIDERATIONS

The deployment of AI raises numerous ethical and legal questions that must be addressed.

Accountability:
- Determining responsibility for decisions made by AI systems, especially in cases of errors or harm, is complex. Questions arise about whether accountability lies with the developers, users, or the AI itself.

Job Displacement:
- Automation driven by AI may lead to job losses in certain sectors, raising concerns about economic inequality and the future of work. Reskilling and upskilling the workforce become critical challenges.

Misinformation and Deepfakes:
- The use of AI to generate convincing fake content poses risks for misinformation, manipulation, and erosion of trust in media.

Explanation:
AI can unintentionally perpetuate or amplify biases present in its training data. This raises ethical questions about fairness, accountability, and inclusivity.

Example:
An AI used for loan approvals might reject applications from minority groups due to biases in historical data, even if the applicants meet the financial requirements.

CHAPTER 11

6   **GENERALIZATION AND TRANSFER LEARNING**

AI models trained in one environment may struggle to generalize their learnings to different contexts.

Limited Generalization:
- A model that performs well on specific tasks or datasets may fail when applied to new situations. This lack of adaptability limits the applicability of AI in dynamic environments.

Transfer Learning Challenges:
- While transfer learning techniques exist to adapt models to new tasks, finding the right approaches to effectively leverage existing knowledge remains an ongoing challenge.

Explanation:
Most AI systems excel in narrow tasks but struggle to generalize across domains. They lack the flexibility of human intelligence.

Example:
An AI trained to play chess cannot apply its knowledge to solve real-world problems, like organizing a team project.

CHAPTER 11

 RESOURCE INTENSITY

Developing and deploying AI solutions can be resource-intensive, requiring significant computational power and energy.

Environmental Impact:
- The energy consumption of training large models can contribute to environmental concerns. Striving for more efficient algorithms and hardware is essential for sustainability.

Economic Barriers:
- High costs associated with AI development can limit access for smaller organizations and startups, leading to disparities in innovation and implementation.

The challenges and limitations of AI underscore the importance of approaching AI development and deployment with caution. Addressing issues related to data quality, bias, interpretability, security, ethics, and resource intensity is crucial for creating responsible AI systems. By understanding these challenges, stakeholders can work towards solutions that maximize the benefits of AI while minimizing potential harms.

CHAPTER 12

Ethics in AI

Ethics in AI

As artificial intelligence continues to advance and integrate into various aspects of society, ethical considerations become increasingly crucial. The deployment of AI systems raises questions about fairness, accountability, transparency, and the societal impacts of these technologies. This chapter explores the ethical implications of AI, highlighting key issues and frameworks to guide responsible development and use.

 **FAIRNESS AND BIAS**

AI systems can inadvertently perpetuate or exacerbate existing biases, leading to unfair treatment of individuals or groups.

Algorithmic Bias:
Bias in AI can arise from skewed training data, flawed assumptions in model design, or biased decision-making processes. This can lead to discriminatory outcomes in areas like hiring, lending, and law enforcement.

Ensuring Fairness:
Ethical AI development requires rigorous testing for biases and implementing strategies to mitigate them. Techniques such as fairness-aware algorithms and diverse training datasets are essential.

CHAPTER 12

2 **ACCOUNTABILITY AND RESPONSIBILITY**

Determining who is accountable for the actions of AI systems poses significant ethical challenges.

Liability Issues:
When AI systems make decisions that result in harm or errors, questions arise about who should be held responsible: the developers, the users, or the AI itself? Establishing clear accountability is critical.

Transparency in Decision-Making:
Providing insights into how AI systems make decisions is essential for accountability. This can involve using explainable AI techniques that allow stakeholders to understand and scrutinize AI processes.

3 **PRIVACY AND DATA PROTECTION**

AI often relies on vast amounts of personal data, raising ethical concerns about privacy and consent.

Informed Consent:
Individuals should be informed about how their data is being used and give explicit consent for its collection and processing. Ethical AI practices prioritize user privacy and data protection.

Data Security:
Safeguarding personal data against breaches and unauthorized access is essential. Organizations must implement robust security measures to protect sensitive information.

CHAPTER 12

 IMPACT ON EMPLOYMENT

The rise of AI and automation presents ethical dilemmas regarding job displacement and economic inequality.

Job Losses:
As AI systems automate tasks traditionally performed by humans, there is a risk of significant job displacement in various sectors. Ethical considerations include how to support affected workers through reskilling and transition programs.

Economic Disparities:
The benefits of AI may not be distributed equitably, potentially widening the gap between those who can leverage AI and those who cannot. Addressing these disparities is an ethical imperative.

 MISINFORMATION AND MANIPULATION

AI technologies can be misused to create misleading content, such as deepfakes and automated misinformation.

Deepfakes:
The ability to create realistic fake videos or audio can lead to manipulation, deception, and erosion of trust in media. Ethical AI development must address the potential for misuse.

Combatting Misinformation:
AI can also be used to detect and counter misinformation. Developing ethical guidelines for the use of AI in media and communication is vital for preserving truth and integrity.

CHAPTER 12

 AUTONOMY AND HUMAN RIGHTS

The deployment of AI must respect individual autonomy and uphold human rights.

Informed Decision-Making:
AI systems should enhance, rather than undermine, human decision-making. Ensuring that individuals retain agency over their choices is a critical ethical consideration.

Upholding Rights:
AI applications should be designed to protect and promote human rights, ensuring that they do not infringe upon freedoms and liberties.

 ENVIRONMENTAL CONSIDERATIONS

The development and operation of AI systems can have environmental impacts, raising ethical concerns about sustainability.

Resource Consumption:
Training large AI models often requires significant computational power, leading to high energy consumption and carbon footprints. Ethical AI development must consider environmental sustainability.

Sustainable Practices:
Organizations should strive to develop energy-efficient algorithms and utilize renewable energy sources in data centers to minimize the ecological impact of AI technologies.

CHAPTER 12

8 ETHICAL FRAMEWORKS AND GUIDELINES

To navigate the complex ethical landscape of AI, several frameworks and guidelines have been proposed.

AI Ethics Principles:
Organizations and governments are developing principles that emphasize fairness, accountability, transparency, privacy, and collaboration in AI development.

Industry Standards:
Collaborations among industry stakeholders can lead to the establishment of ethical standards and best practices for AI deployment.

Regulatory Approaches:
Policymakers are increasingly focused on creating regulations that ensure ethical AI practices while fostering innovation. This involves balancing the need for oversight with the desire to encourage technological advancement.

Ethics in AI is a multifaceted issue that requires careful consideration and proactive measures. Addressing challenges related to fairness, accountability, privacy, and environmental sustainability is essential for developing responsible AI systems that benefit society as a whole. By embracing ethical principles and frameworks, stakeholders can work towards harnessing the power of AI in a manner that aligns with human values and societal well-being.

The Future of AI and Machine Learning

CHAPTER 13

The Future of AI and ML

The field of artificial intelligence and machine learning is evolving rapidly, driven by technological advancements, increased data availability, and growing interest from industries worldwide. As AI continues to develop, it is expected to have profound implications for how we work, live, and interact. This chapter examines the future trends in AI and machine learning, potential advancements, and their societal impacts.

 ## ADVANCEMENTS IN TECHNOLOGY

Several technological advancements are likely to shape the future of AI and machine learning.

Quantum Computing:
Quantum computing has the potential to revolutionize AI by significantly increasing computational power. This could enable the development of more complex algorithms and models that can solve problems currently beyond reach, such as simulating molecular interactions for drug discovery.

Edge Computing:
As IoT devices proliferate, edge computing will become more prevalent. Processing data closer to the source reduces latency and bandwidth usage, allowing AI applications to operate in real-time. This is particularly beneficial for applications in autonomous vehicles, smart cities, and industrial automation.

Natural Language Processing (NLP):
Advances in NLP will lead to more sophisticated conversational agents, translation services, and content generation tools. AI will increasingly understand context, sentiment, and nuances in human language, enabling more meaningful interactions.

CHAPTER 13

2 **ENHANCED PERSONALIZATION**

AI's ability to analyze vast amounts of data will lead to more personalized experiences across various sectors.

Consumer Experiences:
Businesses will leverage AI to provide highly personalized recommendations in e-commerce, entertainment, and advertising. Enhanced customer insights will drive targeted marketing and improve user engagement.

Education:
AI will facilitate personalized learning experiences, adapting educational content and pacing to individual student needs, thereby enhancing educational outcomes.

Healthcare:
Personalized medicine will advance as AI analyzes genetic data and health records, allowing for tailored treatment plans and proactive health management based on individual patient profiles.

CHAPTER 13

 ETHICAL AND RESPONSIBLE AI DEVELOPMENT

As AI becomes more integrated into society, the emphasis on ethical and responsible AI practices will grow.

Regulatory Frameworks:
Governments and organizations will establish regulatory frameworks to ensure AI systems are developed and deployed ethically, addressing issues like bias, accountability, and privacy.

Collaborative Approaches:
Multistakeholder collaborations will emerge, bringing together technologists, ethicists, policymakers, and the public to discuss AI implications and guide its development.

Transparency Initiatives:
There will be a push for greater transparency in AI algorithms and decision-making processes, fostering public trust and understanding of AI systems.

 GLOBAL AI LANDSCAPE

The development of AI will vary across regions, influenced by local needs, regulations, and technological infrastructure.

Emerging Markets:
Countries with growing tech ecosystems will increasingly adopt AI to address unique challenges, such as improving healthcare access, enhancing agricultural productivity, and driving economic growth.

International Cooperation:
As AI becomes a global priority, international collaboration on research, standards, and ethical guidelines will be essential to ensure equitable and beneficial outcomes.

CHAPTER 13

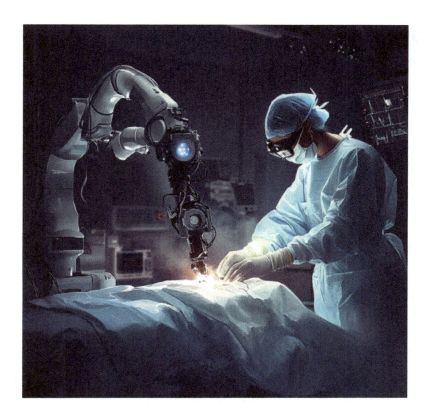

5 **HUMAN-AI COLLABORATION**

The future of AI will increasingly focus on collaboration between humans and machines.

Collaborative Systems:
AI systems will be designed to complement human skills, enhancing decision-making rather than replacing it. This will involve developing intuitive interfaces and tools that allow for seamless human-AI interaction.

Creative Partnerships:
AI will play a role in creative fields, assisting artists, writers, and musicians in generating ideas and exploring new possibilities. The collaboration between human creativity and AI's analytical power will yield innovative outcomes.

CHAPTER 13

6 ## AI IN THE WORKFORCE

The integration of AI into workplaces will transform how tasks are performed and jobs are structured.

Augmented Workforce:
Rather than replacing jobs, AI will augment human capabilities. Employees will work alongside AI systems to enhance productivity and creativity, particularly in fields like design, analysis, and decision-making.

Reskilling Initiatives:
As certain jobs become automated, organizations will invest in reskilling and upskilling their workforce to adapt to new roles created by AI technologies. Continuous learning will become a critical component of career development.

New Job Categories:
The rise of AI will lead to the creation of new job categories, such as AI ethicists, data curators, and algorithm auditors, requiring specialized skills and knowledge.

CHAPTER 13

 BROADER SOCIETAL IMPACTS

The continued advancement of AI and machine learning will have far-reaching effects on society.

Economic Transformation:
AI-driven efficiencies will reshape industries, leading to increased productivity and economic growth. However, this transformation may also create disparities that need to be addressed.

Healthcare Innovations:
AI will drive innovations in healthcare, enabling early disease detection, improved diagnostics, and personalized treatment plans, potentially leading to better health outcomes and longevity.

Environmental Sustainability:
AI can contribute to environmental sustainability through applications in energy management, precision agriculture, and climate modeling, helping address global challenges such as climate change and resource depletion.

The future of AI and machine learning holds immense promise and potential challenges. By embracing advancements in technology, prioritizing ethical practices, and fostering human-AI collaboration, we can harness the power of AI to drive innovation and improve quality of life. Preparing for this future requires a commitment from all stakeholders—technologists, policymakers, educators, and society at large—to shape AI's trajectory in a way that benefits everyone.

CHAPTER 14

Conclusion

CHAPTER 14

Recap of Key Themes

Throughout this book, we have explored the multifaceted world of artificial intelligence (AI) and machine learning (ML), examining their definitions, mechanisms, types, and applications across various sectors. We have also delved into the ethical challenges, limitations, and the future prospects of these transformative technologies. Here, we summarize the key themes discussed in the previous chapters:

Understanding AI and ML:
We began by defining AI and ML, emphasizing how these technologies mimic human intelligence and learn from data. This foundational understanding is crucial for appreciating the complexities and capabilities of AI.

Types of Machine Learning:
We explored supervised, unsupervised, and reinforcement learning, highlighting how different approaches serve various applications, from predictive analytics to clustering and decision-making.

The Role of Data:
We discussed the significance of data as the fuel for AI systems. Quality, quantity, and diversity of data are essential for training effective models that deliver reliable results.

Algorithms as Recipes:
The algorithms that drive machine learning models were examined, showcasing how different techniques are employed to solve specific problems, from linear regression to deep learning.

Real-World Applications:
We highlighted numerous applications of AI across industries, including healthcare, finance, retail, and transportation, demonstrating the transformative impact of AI on everyday life and business operations.

CHAPTER 14

Ethics and Challenges:
The ethical considerations of AI, including bias, accountability, privacy, and environmental impact, were critical topics. We emphasized the need for responsible AI development and adherence to ethical frameworks.

The Future of AI:
Finally, we looked ahead to the future of AI and machine learning, discussing potential advancements, the importance of human-AI collaboration, and the societal implications of widespread AI adoption.

CHAPTER 14

→ THE PATH FORWARD

As we conclude this exploration of AI and machine learning, it is essential to reflect on the path forward. The potential of AI to enhance our lives is immense, but so too are the responsibilities that come with it. Here are some key considerations for the future:

Fostering Innovation:
Continued investment in AI research and development is crucial. Innovators should focus on creating solutions that address real-world problems while considering the ethical implications of their work.

CHAPTER 14

Promoting Inclusivity:
As AI technologies evolve, ensuring that their benefits are accessible to all is paramount. This includes promoting diversity in AI development teams and engaging with underrepresented communities to address their unique challenges.

Building Trust:
Transparency and explainability in AI systems are vital for building public trust. Stakeholders must commit to developing AI that is understandable and accountable, allowing users to feel secure in its use.

Collaboration Across Sectors:
The challenges posed by AI are complex and multifaceted. Collaborative efforts among governments, academia, industry, and civil society will be essential to create comprehensive strategies for addressing ethical, legal, and societal issues.

Adapting to Change:
As AI continues to advance, individuals and organizations must be prepared to adapt. Continuous learning and reskilling will become increasingly important as job roles evolve and new opportunities arise.

CHAPTER 14

→ **FINAL THOUGHTS**

Artificial intelligence and machine learning represent a pivotal shift in how we understand and interact with technology. As we stand on the brink of this new era, it is our collective responsibility to guide the development of AI in a way that maximizes its benefits while minimizing risks. By embracing ethical principles, fostering innovation, and prioritizing human well-being, we can harness the full potential of AI to create a brighter, more equitable future.

The journey of AI and machine learning is just beginning. As we move forward, let us remain curious, thoughtful, and proactive in shaping a future where technology serves humanity and enhances our quality of life. Together, we can navigate the challenges and seize the opportunities that AI presents, ensuring it becomes a force for good in our world.

www.ingramcontent.com/pod-product-compliance
Lightning Source LLC
LaVergne TN
LVHW081530050326
832903LV00025B/1711